Under the Sea
Barracudas

by Deborah Nuzzolo

Consulting Editor: Gail Saunders-Smith, PhD

Consultant: Ray Davis
Senior Vice President, Zoological Operations
Georgia Aquarium

Mankato, Minnesota

Pebble Plus is published by Capstone Press,
151 Good Counsel Drive, P.O. Box 669, Mankato, Minnesota 56002.
www.capstonepress.com

1 2 3 4 5 6 12 11 10 09 08 07

Library of Congress Cataloging-in-Publication Data
Nuzzolo, Deborah.
    Barracudas / by Deborah Nuzzolo.
    p.cm.—(Pebble plus. Under the sea)
    Summary: "Simple text and photographs describe barracudas, their body parts, and what they do"—
Provided by publisher.
    Includes bibliographical references and index.
    ISBN-13: 978-1-4296-0032-3 (hardcover)
    ISBN-10: 1-4296-0032-2 (hardcover)
    1. Barracudas—Juvenile literature. I. Title. II. Series.
QL638.S77N89 2008
597'.7—dc22   2006101732

Editorial Credits
Mari Schuh, editor; Juliette Peters, set designer; Kim Brown, book designer; Charlene Deyle, photo researcher

Photos Credits
Bruce Coleman Inc./M. Timothy O'Keefe, 18–19; V&W/Masa Ushioda, 13
Corbis/zefa/Photex/E. Bradley, cover
Marty Snyderman, 4–5
Minden Pictures/HIROYA MINAKUCHI, 16–17
SeaPics, 6–7, 8–9, 15
Shutterstock/Lawrence Cruciana, 20–21; Sergey Popov, 1
Tom Stack & Associates, Inc./Brian Parker, 10–11

Note to Parents and Teachers

The Under the Sea set supports national science standards related to the diversity
and unity of life. This book describes and illustrates barracudas. The images support
early readers in understanding the text. The repetition of words and phrases helps early
readers learn new words. This book also introduces early readers to subject-specific
vocabulary words, which are defined in the Glossary section. Early readers may need
assistance to read some words and to use the Table of Contents, Glossary, Read More,
Internet Sites, and Index sections of the book.

Table of Contents

What Are Barracudas?

Barracudas are
long, thin fish
with strong teeth.

Small barracudas
are as long as a pillow.
Big barracudas
are as long as a bed.

Body Parts

Barracudas have
big mouths.
Their mouths have
sharp teeth.

Smooth silver scales
cover barracudas.

Barracudas have fins
for swimming.

fins

Strong tails help
barracudas swim fast.

What Barracudas Do

Small barracudas swim
in groups called schools.
Big barracudas swim alone.

Barracudas look for prey
with their large eyes.
They snap up small fish.

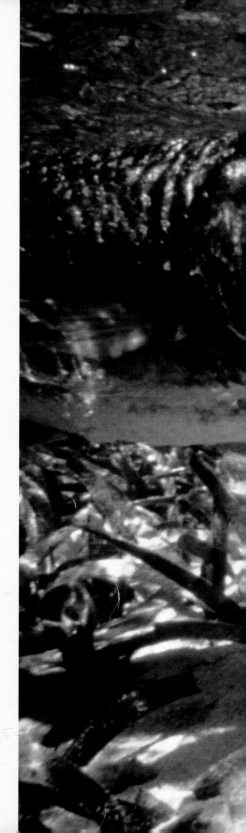

Under the Sea

Barracudas swim

in warm or cool waters

under the sea.

Glossary

fin—a body part that fish use to swim and steer

fish—a cold-blooded animal that lives in water and has scales, fins, and gills

prey—an animal hunted by another animal for food; barracudas hunt small fish.

scale—a hard, protective body covering for a fish; barracudas have smooth silver scales.

school—a group of fish swimming together

snap up—to grab quickly

Read More

Carson, Mary Kay. *In the Deep.* Science Links. Philadelphia: Chelsea Clubhouse, 2003.

Dahl, Michael. *One Giant Splash: A Counting Book about the Ocean.* Know Your Numbers. Minneapolis: Picture Window Books, 2004.

Richardson, Adele. *Fish.* First Facts: Exploring the Animal Kingdom. Mankato, Minn.: Capstone Press, 2005.

Internet Sites

FactHound offers a safe, fun way to find Internet sites related to this book. All of the sites on FactHound have been researched by our staff.

Here's how:

1. Visit *www.facthound.com*

2. Choose your grade level.

3. Type in this book ID **1429600322** for age-appropriate sites. You may also browse subjects by clicking on letters, or by clicking on pictures and words.

4. Click on the **Fetch It** button.

FactHound will fetch the best sites for you!

Index

Word Count: 83
Grade: 1
Early-Intervention Level: 14